My Journey

With God

Giving People Hope in a Fallen World

Rebecca Kilwin

Christy Smith, Editor

Copyright © Rebecca Kilwin

All rights reserved. No part of this book may be used or reproduced by any means, graphic, electronic, or mechanical, including photocopying, recording, or taping or by any information storage retrieval system without the written permission of the publisher except in the case of brief quotations embodied in critical articles and reviews.

Because of the dynamic nature of the Internet, any web addresses or links contained in this book may have changed since publication and may no longer be valid. The views expressed in this work are solely those of the author and do not necessarily reflect the views of the publisher, and the publisher hereby disclaims any responsibility for them.

ISBN-13: 979-8-218-34856-4

Printed in the United States of America

Publication Date: 12/30/2023

TABLE OF CONTENTS

Chapter 1	My Birth	1
Chapter 2	Daddy's Little Girl	4
Chapter 3	Honor Your Mother And Father	7
Chapter 4	Our Refuge	10
Chapter 5	Bitterness Equals Unforgiveness	15
Chapter 6	Rebellion Is Not The Answer	17
Chapter 7	Depression Should Not Be Ignored	21
Chapter 8	Promise Keeper	24
Chapter 9	God's Wisdom	27
Chapter 10	God's Favor	32

TABLE OF CONTENTS
(Continued)

Chapter 11	Forgiveness	33
Chapter 12	Endless Provision	37
Chapter 13	Guilt Is Meant To Teach Us	40
Chapter 14	Love And Marriage	44
Chapter 15	Anger	47
Chapter 16	Anxiety	49
Chapter 17	Healer	55
Chapter 18	Be Intentional	62
Chapter 19	Denial	65
Chapter 20	When Our Faith is Tested	67

TABLE OF CONTENTS
(Continued)

Chapter 21	Stay Humble	70
Chapter 22	Way Maker	72
Chapter 23	Our Identity Is In Christ	75
Chapter 24	The Positive Side Of Covid	80
Chapter 25	A Second Chance To Change Your Final Answer	83

My Challenge and The Moral	86
Updates	87
Stay Tuned!	90
About The Author	91

My Journey With God | Rebecca Kilwin

INTRODUCTION

Welcome to my journey with God. My prayer is the testimonies will inspire you to reflect upon where your relationship is with God. Inspire you to step out of your comfort zone and live the life He has for you. He promised to provide for our needs and help us overcome the trials of this earthly life.

"I have told you these things, so that you may have peace…In this world you will have trouble…But take heart I have overcome the world."

(John 16:3 NIV)

So come along with me... as I share my story.

DISCLAIMER

I have a lot to say. The names and identities will remain unknown to protect the innocent. Hopefully, it is well worth the read. My alias is Becky, Beckmiester, Beck, Becks, Becky-Boo.

Chapter 1
My Birth

One year, long ago, I was born and diagnosed with Turner's Syndrome. I did not have all my growth and reproductive chromosomes. The first couple of years of my life were touch and go. I would turn blue, swell up like a balloon, and didn't keep anything down. My mom and dad were given three options; to die, stay the size of a baby my whole adult life, or be mentally retarded.

Remember, this was a year-long ago. Retardation was never in the diagnosis. I am 4 11 ½, thank you very much. Making the doctors give me credit for that ½ inch must have paid off. I recently discovered if I stand on my tippy-toes I can reach the bottom of the washing machine.

"For you created my inmost being you knit me together in my mother's womb."

(Psalm 139:13 NIV)

I praise you because I am fearfully and wonderfully made. Ninety percent of all babies born with Turner's Syndrome self-abort. If you go by science; there is no reason for me to be here. There were a lot of people praying for me.

"For when two or three are gathered in my name, there I am with them."

(Matthew 18:20 NIV)

Chapter 2
Daddy's Little Girl

My Dad served in Vietnam, worked at my grandfather's service station since he was 16 years old, and worked two jobs to make ends meet, tells me he was proud of me, was generous with his money, and "tried" to teach me to drive. I mean, a garage wall, several parked cars, mailboxes, and numerous accidents. I'm guessing the whole dead stop on the highway to change lanes thing <u>was a bit much</u>!

The Children's Palace wall was not my fault! He had a lot of patience with me. He took up auctioneering. It was so much fun being a runner.

My parents got divorced and he re-married. I don't remember how old I was when this happened. Dad has retired and moved to another State. I am proud and happy for them. He worked hard his whole life.

I outgrew my "Daddy's Little Girl" shirt and cried for days because it made me feel special. Recently, he bought me a shirt that says, "My daughters are never too old to be Daddy's Little Girl." I thought, *'I want a shirt from my Heavenly Father, that says "Daddy's Little Girl."'* God offers us so much more than a t-shirt. He offers salvation, forgiveness, mercy and grace, and eternity with Him in Heaven. I long to hear the words, "Well done good and faithful servant."

"Well done my good and faithful servant. Come and share in my happiness."

(Matthew 25:21 NIV)

Chapter 3
Honor Your Mother And Father

Learning new things and making friends was hard for me. The struggle to feel accepted was real. I decided running away was a good idea and packed up a laundry basket.

My mom's response was, "I'm sorry you feel that way. I'll help you pack."

I sat on the porch crying for hours. My sister, (she will not be getting an alias; she can sit on me.), and I would sit at the doorway of our bedrooms refusing to make amends. Sometimes for several days.

Eventually we "grudgingly made amends".

I was an office runner in High School. The teasing was relentless. Coming home in tears became a frequent occurrence.

My mom would say, "God makes good things in small packages."

I told her my junior year I was dropping out of high school.

"And you're living where?" she asked.

I guess I am going to school! The counselor said I was a half credit short of graduating "No matter what courses I took." The fear of getting teased kept me from attending my graduation.

I have not given my mom enough credit. She took me in as an adult, watched the kids, and could have made a different choice when I was born. Jesus demonstrated this on the cross.

"Jesus therefore, seeing his mother and the disciple, whom he loved, standing by, said, "Woman behold thy Son." Then he said to the disciple, "Behold thy mother." And from that hour the disciple took her into his own home."

(John 25:7 NIV)

Chapter 4
Our Refuge

When I was seventeen a twenty-five-year-old man bought me alcohol, took me to his apartment, and raped me. It took me days to tell the counselor at school. She encouraged me to tell my mom. I felt dirty, ashamed, and violated. Questioned if I had imagined it. Wondered if there were other victims.

My mom was on the phone. She took one look at my face and abruptly ended her conversation. I was too scared to identify the apartment. It wasn't as violent as it could have been. No weapons, or anything like that. Thank the Lord!

"The Lord also will be a refuge for the oppressed, refuge in times of trouble."

(Psalm 9:9 NIV)

After dropping my niece and nephew off at my sister's, I had an accident with a semi-truck. I lost consciousness and my whole life flashed before my eyes. My boyfriend at the time had just traded in his smaller car for a larger one. The police said, "You are lucky to be alive and didn't go under that truck. It dragged you across the entire overpass." It took months to recover.

"The Lord will keep you from all harm—He will watch over your life; the Lord will watch over your coming and going both now and forevermore."
(Psalm 121: 7-8 NIV)

One night working at the Olive Garden. I lost my pocketbook with the money and receipts. It took an hour to find it. The manager wrote me up. I left later than normal.

They got robbed shortly after I left. My coworkers had to put their heads down on the bar.

The robbers shot holes in the office and locked them in the basement until the next morning. How traumatized would I have been?

"My God, my rock, in whom I take refuge, my shield, and the horn of my salvation, my stronghold and my refuge, my savior; you save me from violence. I call upon the Lord, who is worthy to be praised, and I am saved from my enemies."
(2 Samuel: 22-3-4 NIV)

Driving home one night, the ball joint went out on the car and I hit a guard rail. Let the record show <u>it was not my fault</u>! The officer said it was clear I was not speeding.

Driving home, a car ran a red light and spun me across three lanes of traffic. Nearly hitting an electrical box. I had two foster children in the car with me, one of them was bleeding.

I was shaken up. He was okay, praise the Lord. My wrist was broken. It took numerous months to heal from all the bruising from the seat belt and airbag. Not all the accidents <u>were my fault</u>!

Chapter 5
Bitterness Equals Unforgiveness

I married the boyfriend whose car I was driving when I had the semi-truck accident. He was controlling and tried to hit me. I ducked and he punched a hole in the wall. Because I accidentally washed a check that was in his pocket, he pulled the spark plugs out of my car to keep me from leaving.

He had an affair with my "best friend" and I got a venereal disease. The only way to treat it was to put acid on my hum hum. I felt betrayed, angry, resentful, and hurt. I confronted my "friend" and almost got arrested. Oh, the bitter tears I cried! We divorced and I moved back in with my mom.

"Get rid of all bitterness, rage, and anger, brawling and slander, along with every form of malice."

(Ephesians 4:31 NIV)

Chapter 6
Rebellion Is Not The Answer

I became very rebellious. Dating any man that paid attention to me. It often became intimate. I started hanging with anyone my mom said not to, skipping classes, and experimenting with marijuana. Basically, I did whatever I wanted to do.

"Why do you call me Lord and not do what I tell you?"

(Luke 6:46 NIV)

My "Ah Ha" moment came when I chose to get drunk and drive. I ran a red light nearly causing a horrific (potentially fatal) accident.

"Be sober, be vigilant because, the devil, as a roaring lion, walketh about seeking whom he may devour."

(1 Peter 5:6 NIV)

No more alcohol for me! I began my weight loss journey and signed up for early childhood classes. No doubt this was all in God's plan.

"The Lord is slow to anger, abounding in love and forgiving in sin and rebellion."
>   (Numbers 14:18 NIV)

Next stop. The wonderful land of restaurant management. (highly overrated.) This guy worked next door and would come to talk to me. We began to date and got married. The beginning of our marriage included my grandmother being diagnosed with breast cancer and given six months to live. Her alias is Spiritual Warrior.

My thyroid level was at 35 (normal is seven), and my sister

was abducted, beaten, and left for dead in a field.

His uncle was murdered and found dead at the bottom of a lake, and we were trying to move into a rental house.

I began to ask myself, 'Why is all of this happening to me? *'What is wrong with me?'*

"For I know the plans I have for you." Declares the Lord, "Plans to prosper you and not to harm you, plans to give you hope and a future."

(Jeremiah 29:11 NIV)

Chapter 7
Depression Should Not Be Ignored

After the move, I got diagnosed with severe depression and was put on antidepressants. The choice to take too many was no good! Severe lockjaw set in. I could not even open my mouth to call for help. God revealed himself that day.

'I am the Alpha and Omega. The giver and taker of life. It is not your right to take it. I am not done with you yet.'

I remember going to my Spiritual Leader after the semi-accident.

"I'm scared because I know I am going to be standing before God one day. I have made bad choices."

"Don't worry Beck, God will only see the snow-white blood of Jesus," she answered.

"How will I know if I am saved?" I asked.

"You will want to shout it from the rooftops."

Instantly, my mouth opened, and I cried, "Oh God, what have I done?" I jumped up and started dancing around the house.

"And free those who all their lives have been held in slavery by their fear of death."

(Hebrews 2:15 NIV)

Chapter 8
Promise Keeper

I didn't realize how strong my desire to have children was. I took three positive pregnancy tests, but the Dr. said I wasn't pregnant. I went to church crying and brokenhearted. In honor of my Spiritual Warrior, we will say the name "Rascal" came to mind.

"Be still and know that I am God," I heard inwardly. The first of <u>many</u> conversations between God and me.

"The Lord is close to the brokenhearted and saves the crushed in spirit."

(Psalm 34:18 NIV)

We began the tedious task of becoming foster parents. Six years and eleven foster children later we got placed with a three-month-old baby girl. The supervisor said she would be going home by the end of the week.

Her alias is Love Bug. Several weeks later I stood in the kitchen, "God I don't know how much heartache I can take."

"Be still and know that I am God," He reminded me. I was reminded, too, of the name "Rascal." The next week I got a call from the social worker.

"I have a three-day-old baby boy. He's a legal risk. Do you want him?" *'Did I want him?'*

I almost hung up on her without getting the details. Not to mention calling my ex-husband. In my defense, I was super excited! On the way to pick him up, I kept telling myself, "Down Girl." The social worker put this 4lb 7oz baby in my hands. I thought, *'What if I break him?'* I asked his name.

"He doesn't have one. Did you have one in mind?" *'Did I have one in mind?'*

His name is Rascal! Rascal's adoption was finalized the same year. Love Bug's adoption was finalized when she was 3 ½. Twice blessed!

"He settles the childless woman in her home as the happy mother of children. Praise the Lord!"
(Psalm 113 NIV)

Chapter 9
God's Wisdom

I began to see signs of sexual abuse in Love Bug. It still breaks my heart. I told my ex-husband, "I am concerned about Love Bug. I am going to make an appointment with the play therapist. "Well, Love Bug and Rascal were under the covers together." WHAT? She was showing more signs. We stayed at my sister's house.

During a counseling session, my ex-husband stated, "I am angry because I feel like you are accusing me. I told him if that were the case, I would have signed the lease on the apartment I got approved for. I was trying to get to the bottom of it. My ex-husband blurted out, "I will tell you this "love bug" touched me down there but I told her it was not okay." <u>Wait back it up! What</u>??

The lease was signed, and my priorities were filing for a divorce and bankruptcy.

At work, the director said, "You don't have to pay tuition anymore."

"Why?" I asked.

"Do not look a gift horse in the mouth." The worker said, "They cannot charge you tuition. They have a contract with the state. I already told her that." she replied.

I began to think about all the tuition I had paid. My 4:00 a.m. mission Should I choose to accept it? Find those receipts! Mission accomplished!

I was terrified of losing my job. I approached her. "I feel I am entitled to this money."

"Let me talk to the owner," she answered.

The owner said, "What is right is right. Let me talk to my attorney."

The director informed me they did not keep receipts for that long. I handed her mine. The owner reimbursed me over five thousand dollars. I filed for divorce and bankruptcy.

"Put on the whole armor of God, that ye may be able to stand against the wiles of the devil."
(Ephesians 6:11 NIV)

Chapter 10
God's Favor

My ex-husband accused me of having a boyfriend, not letting him see Love Bug and Rascal. He said he wanted the car, even though he did not have a license. He did not owe me child support. My attorney told him he did as well as back child support! We agreed that he would not pay child support if he gave up his parental rights.

"Do you feel this is in the best interest of your children?" the judge asked.

I looked him in the eyes and said, "Yes, your honor I really do!" At that moment, he smiled, and I received the favor I had prayed for.

"For whoever finds me finds life and favor from the Lord."

(Proverbs 8:35 NIV)

Chapter 11
Forgiveness

Forgiving my ex-husband was hard. "How do I forgive the unforgivable?" I asked God.

"Haven't I forgiven you?" He reminded me.
Not the answer I expected!

"Be kind to one another, as God in Christ forgave you."

(Ephesians 4:32 NIV)

Asking forgiveness from God, the person you wronged, and forgiving yourself is crucial.

"Then I acknowledged my sin to you and did not cover up my iniquity, I said, "I will confess my transgressions to the Lord, and you forgave the guilt of my sin."

(Psalm 3:25 NIV)

We all need forgiveness. God already knows what we need forgiveness for. Forgiving others does not mean forgetting. Forgiving will free us from a lifetime of guilt, anger, bitterness, hate, physical, mental, and spiritual issues.

"For all have sinned and fallen short of the glory of God."

(Romans 3:23 NIV)

Jesus demonstrated the importance of forgiveness on the cross.

"When they came to the place called the Skull, there they were crucified, Him and the criminals, one on the right and the other on the left. But Jesus was saying, "Father, forgive them for they do not know what they are doing."

(Luke 23: 33-34 NIV)

Chapter 12
Endless Provision

After the divorce, we moved from a two-bedroom apartment to a three-bedroom with less rent. I found a better job with benefits, received grants to continue my classes, food assistance, help from family, and Medicaid. The school sent gifts that filled our living room and free childcare. My hours got drastically cut. We were facing eviction!

My dad called, "God put it on my heart to send you $1,000 I am putting it in the mail today." My pride almost left us homeless.

When I was with my ex-husband, I would pray for money to pay the bills. After I closed my Bible the phone would ring, and he would get called in on his day off or early. This happened numerous times. He asked me to stop praying.

"Um no."

My Mom and sisters would bring us groceries, watch the kids, help pick them up when I worked late, and give us money.

My dad would give us money and take us to a theme park in another state. He paid for car repairs and helped pay for the divorce. My great-aunt sent us money after one of the accidents.

"And My God will supply all of your needs according to his riches and glory."
(Philippians 4:19 NIV)

Chapter 13
Guilt Is Meant To Teach Us

I would get daily calls from Rascals Elementary School and daycares. He was aggressively damaging property, threatening and hurting others. He began to display these behaviors at home.

Numerous hospitalizations, play therapy, intensive in-home therapy, psychiatrist, psychologist, in-patient treatment programs, and a summer at a youth ranch.

I did not discipline them and set the best example. Guilt played a huge role in my parenting choices.

> "Train a child up in the way he should go; even when he is old, he will not depart from it.'"
>
> (Proverbs 22:6 NIV)

I played favoritism. Love Bug got the short end of the stick. I apologized, and we have a healthy relationship now. Can I change what has already been done? NO! I can change my future choices, reactions, and attitude. Learn from my sin.

I was always looking down with clenched teeth and hands, unable to look people in the eye, apologizing unnecessarily, and feeling guilty even when I was not.

I got pulled over for running a red light.

"Um Mom, you're going to jail!" the kids exclaimed.

The officer put his hands on his hips and asked, "Ma'am, what makes them think you are going to jail today?" I thought, *"Seriously? There are four. Okay, I did it just take me away!"* It had been a long and rough day.

I felt guilty about what Love Bug and Rascal have been through. As I was looking over the book, I felt a twinge of guilt because I realized a lot of it revolves around Rascal.

"Those who look to Him are radiant and their faces shall never be ashamed."

      (Psalm 34:5 NIV)

Chapter 14
Love And Marriage

I met this guy online. We will call him, "THE HEAD RASCAL." We began to date, and I got scared of getting hurt again. My prayer was, *'God if this is not Your will, let it end. I cannot do it without You.'*

Rascal asked if Head Rascal could come over and watch Star Wars. That's when I felt comfortable inviting Head Rascal over. We got married at the courthouse and Lovebug exclaimed, "I have a daddy now!"

Sorry to my parents and in-laws, we were not honest about the way we met. Head Rascal and I are fifteen years apart. His parents were married for over 56 years. His mom cooked homemade meals every day. They spent a lot of family time together. He was raised Catholic and did not have children.

My parents are divorced, and I have been cooking my own meals since I was seventeen. I attended a non-denominational church and adopted two children. It has been VERY hard to find a compromise.

I cannot speak for Head Rascal. I was struggling with lust, anxiety, bulimia, loneliness, financial issues, and enabling others. Anything to fill the void.

"But soon thereafter, there emerged a seeming contradiction: "The Lord God said, "It is not good that man shall be alone. I will make a helper suitable for him." (Genesis 2:18 NIV)

We were not meant to do life alone!

Chapter 15
Anger

Head Rascal and Rascal butt heads all the time. I am always the mediator. I am angry with myself because I enabled them to think this behavior is acceptable. I am angry that they put me in this position. They intentionally push each other's buttons and say mean and hurtful things. Wow! I have a lot of unresolved anger. It is time to let it go. This is not easy. Better than holding it in and letting it fester.

"My dear brothers and sisters, take note of this. Everyone

should be quick to listen, slow to speak, and slow to become angry. Because this does not produce the righteousness that God desires."

(James 1: 19-20 NIV)

Chapter 16
Anxiety

Having to be the mediator between Head Rascal and Rascal certainly added more stress. Worrying about the consequences of their actions. They feed off of each other. I had to let Rascal experience the consequences of his actions. I have struggled with anxiety my whole life. I worried about things before they happened. Sometimes they never did. I took it out of God's hands and expected perfection from myself.

"Have I not commanded you? Be strong and courageous. Do not be afraid; do not be discouraged; for the Lord, your God will be with you wherever you may go."

(Joshua 1:9 NIV)

I was being harassed by a coworker. I had talked to the director about a situation. She would follow me in the bathroom, "You are going to pay for this." On the playground and in the classrooms. Comment after comment. The director's solution was to "separate us for a while." That did not work because she found a way. On my way to work, I said, *'Please God if only she could get a flat tire. I do not want her sick or hurt.'*

I got to the intersection of work. My tire sensor went off. "Vengeance is mine sayeth the Lord." I bet you thought I was going to say I had another accident. Just an attitude check and proof of God's understanding and even humor.

"But even if you suffer for doing what is right, God will reward you for it. So do not worry or be afraid of their threats." (1 Peter 3:14 NIV)

I continued to get daily calls. Rascal was being

aggressive, damaging property and threatening people.

After numerous hospitalizations, play therapy, psychiatrists, psychologists, intensive in-home therapy, case workers from school, hospitals, and the state, the Department of Mental Health, and an entire summer at a youth ranch, we have had to call the police. He threatened to burn our house down with a lighter in his hand, kick my face in, and break everything in the house if I took his phone away.

Rascal destroyed our rental house; put huge holes in walls, shattered the front door, and broke numerous things, sometimes on purpose, that he knew were sentimental to Head

Rascal. He broke down our bedroom door to get what we had taken from him. He also broke my nose and left huge bruises and scratches.

Rascal refuses to go to school, saying, "You can't make me.". He is right in the sense I cannot get a DJO because he had to commit a crime for that to happen.

The police and courts have given me the runaround; shifting the blame! He has more than proven he is capable of committing a crime. Are we supposed to wait for him to burn the house down?

He is currently hospitalized because he was hitting me and broke down our front door frame and all. There are no consequences for his actions. Sometimes experience is the best teacher. I have to prayerfully decide where to go from here. He is still a minor. By God's mercy and grace, the seed was planted.

"Train up a child in the way he should go; even when he is old, he will not depart from it."
(Proverbs 22:6 NIV)

Chapter 17
Healer

My medical history includes (singing to the tune The Twelve Days of Christmas.): Tonsillectomy, Appendectomy, Gall Bladder Surgery, Back Surgery, Hysterectomy, Sinus Surgery, Bladder Suspension, Turners Syndrome, Attention Deficit Disorder, High Blood Pressure, High Cholesterol, Depression, Anxiety, Obesity, Anemia, Sleep Apnea, Hypothyroidism, severe Acid Reflux, and environmental allergies. Thyroid Biopsy /Cancer Scare. Two words for a thyroid biopsy and a cortisone shot in my back on the same day. OUCH! And OOUUCCHH! Numerous ER and Urgent-Care visits.

I was admitted to the hospital for gastroenterology issues, pneumonia, and dehydration. Head Rascal, Rascal, and I got Covid. I am sure I left things out.

"Behold, I will bring it health and cure them, and will reveal unto them the abundance of peace and truth."

(Jeremiah 33:6 NIV)

When Rascal was two, he ran high fevers. He said, "I don't feel good." We went to the pediatrician and I expressed my concern he felt his stomach, "He has the flu and should be okay." That night he woke up with a high fever and winced when I touched him.

My heart said this is not the flu. The ER doctor said, "It is the flu we will observe him for a couple of hours and send him home." It was <u>nine hours later</u> when they began to discharge him!

"How old is this baby?" a new on-shift doctor asked. I told her he was two years old.

"I do not feel comfortable sending him home. He is in pain.

I want to send him to Children's Hospital." The doctor declared. At Children's Hospital, the CT scan revealed a ruptured appendix.

I laid my hand on him and prayed, *'God, I can't believe you blessed me with this baby to take him from me now.'* The first night was in the ICU. He spent two weeks in the hospital and was sent home with a pic line so I could give him antibiotics at home.

My brother-in-law was diagnosed with stage three thoracic cancer. He endured radiation and chemo treatments. I cannot imagine how brutal they were. His last two scans revealed no signs of cancer at all. They have five beautiful children. They were starting to plan for his death.

"Oh no, this is going to be your testimony!" But another example of God's healing powers.

"Heal me oh Lord, and I shall be saved, for You are my praise."

(Jeremiah 17:14 NIV)

Last year I went to the emergency room thinking I was having a seizure. It turned out I was having convulsions from anxiety. I was overwhelmed by being laid off, and rioting at the Capital.

"For the Spirit of God does not make us timid, but gives us power, love, and self-control."
(2 Timothy NIV)

Before my back surgery, I was terrified of falling. My co-worker said, "Do not worry, you might fall, but you will always get back up." I thought that was a weird thing to say.

"For though the righteous man falls seven times, he will rise again, but the wicked stumble into calamity."

(Proverbs 24:16 NIV)

Chapter 18
Be Intentional

Prioritizing: God, head rascal, love bug, rascal, family, friends, job, basically loving others. When Head Rascal wakes up still angry, I get his orange juice, say good morning, and greet him with a kiss. Even though, I want to bop him in the head with a skillet.

"Above all, love each other deeply, because love covers a multitude of sins." I tried it on Love Bug, Rascal, and coworkers. Pretending like I did not know they were angry with me.

(1 Peter 7:8 NIV)

When I wrong somebody, I intentionally apologize. I leave my phone at home when we go to church. I like the coloring app on my phone and tablet. I put them in the bedroom.

"You need to persevere so that when you have done the will of God, you will receive what he has promised."

(Hebrews 10:36 NIV)

It is hard for me to sit still long enough to hear what God is saying to me. I read my Bible and a devotional. The more I practice, the easier it becomes. This has strengthened my faith and spiritual growth.

"Listen to me; be silent, and I will teach you wisdom."

(Job 33:33 NIV)

Chapter 19
Denial

I was in denial about several things. People ask, "Are you ok?" I say I am when I'm not. I tell myself things are under control when they are out of control.

I was in denial that at times I was mad at God. Sometimes I felt completely abandoned by him. There were times I failed to seek Him and His will. I was in denial about being humble, anxious, and at times depressed. I am starting to think more about material things than I should.

"Then Jesus said to his disciples, "If anyone would come after me, let him deny himself pick up their cross and follow me."

(Matthew 16:24 NIV)

I had prejudice in my heart, and thoughts about a lot of minority groups. I have to still work on this. I am better about owning it.

"In whom ye are also built together for one habitation of God through the Spirit."

(Ephesians 2:22 NIV)

Chapter 20
When Our Faith Is Tested

The last thing I need to do is stray away from God. Rascal came back home from the hospital. I am waiting for a biopsy result that was sent to another state.

They are redoing the test in three months. My thyroid medication dosage has been changed four times. The fear of losing my job is trying to creep its way back in. I tripped over a cot and fell against a utility cart; my grandmother passed away.

Phone calls and emails from doctors, schools, potential

residential treatment for Rascal, social workers, and counselors.

I had to reschedule the second interview for a summer job because the check engine light came on in the car. The car was old, the passenger door would not open from the guardrail accident, and we invested a lot of money in repairs.

I fell again and got a concussion. My friend at church lost her twenty-year-old granddaughter to violence. My heart is breaking for them.

"And let us hold unswervingly to the hope we profess. For He who promised is faithful."
            (Hebrews 10:23 NIV)

Chapter 21
Stay Humble

Being humble is not a specialty of mine. People would compliment me on my creativity, wittiness, walk with God, compassion for other people, and patience. My brother-in-law once told me, "You have the patience of Job."

At church, a social worker told me, "I have been watching your family. Your daughter was at the altar praying with someone, you, your husband, and your son were serving communion. Excellent job."

Love Bug wrote me a letter, "I know I do not say it enough but thank you for adopting me. You may have missed a few things. You taught us how to love one another and treat each other like human beings along with common sense." My former coworkers said I was a great example daily of how to live a Christian life. A foster daughter wrote me a letter saying she knew when she came; she would never be the same.

At recognition ceremonies, I would be upset if I did not get recognition. I even thought, "Why should I bother?"

"The reward for humility and fear of the Lord is riches and honor and life."

(Proverbs 22:24 NIV)

Chapter 22
Way Maker

I found residential treatment for Rascal. He is going there, and we are trying to get on a waiting list for independent living. He is currently in another residential treatment program. He has a job and we bought him a bike for transportation. Even though, he does not know how to ride one.

We moved to a bigger rental house. With room for us to spread out, our own shower, and my A-Z man. I call Head Rascal my A-Z man because he has everything from A-Z. On our first Christmas together, I went to the dollar store and bought stocking stuffers from A-Z.

Did I mention we have **our own shower**? After over twenty years of community college, I got my teaching certificate. Who knew they stopped giving financial aid after twenty years? The last job was the worst I have ever experienced. Teachers were yelling loudly at the kids, putting babies in cribs for time out, and walking completely out of the room, leaving them unattended. I was left outside with twos, threes, toddlers, and school agers.

I talked to the owner. She made it miserable for me. Everything was my fault and never good or clean enough. She would yell at me. I got blessed with a job in the school district and quit. I took away something from that job. Phonics learning, perseverance and I am more mindful to clean as I go.

We took some tax money and bought a car. I got a summer job! With inflation car payments and gas prices. It could not have come at a better time.

"Where there is no way, Jesus is the way, the truth, and the life. God sent his word to heal and save you from all your destructions."

(Psalm 107:20 NIV)

Chapter 23
Our Identity is in Christ

Periodically, I emailed the social worker about Love Bug's siblings. This was her response, "I have been going over old emails and came across the one regarding your daughter. They are open to reuniting. Here is the information."

I called and it was a great conversation. Love Bug was questioning what her birth mother looked like. "I know you are my mom. I just want to see if I look like her."

I texted the mom and said, "I know it is a busy time of year, Christmas, Love Bug, and her sister's birthday. I was wondering what the possibility of getting together is?"

"How does Saturday sound?" was her reply.

We met at McDonald's and discovered not only did we live in the same city, but Love Bug had gone to middle school with her sister. I need to clarify; this was not her birth mom but a friend of the family who adopted her siblings.

Rascal disclosed to me that he was gay. I told him, "You know that I am a Christian and do not approve of that lifestyle. God did not approve of my three marriages. That is between you and God."

> "So then, each of us will give an account of ourselves to God."
>
> (Romans 14:12 NIV)

I have always struggled with my weight, obesity at times. Felt no self-worth, how could anyone love me, and that bulimia was the answer. The reality is I bought into the lie that the way I look and the things I do were going to gain my citizenship in heaven.

My journey included Weight Watchers, Jenny Craig, sporadic exercise, and Zumba. I lost fifty pounds (found it.) Lost sixty pounds (found that too.) When I started focusing on getting healthier; I lost fifty pounds (It is still missing ish!) Doing Zumba in moderation, portion control, and making better food choices. Being hard on myself if I "blew it" and dieting was not an option! I like chocolate, ice cream, and cheesecake. <u>I really like cheesecake.</u>

After my grandfather passed away, I found out he was not my biological grandfather. Whoa so --- <u>is not</u> my maiden name!

When I was younger, I thought I was adopted. I don't look like my mom and sisters. That is until my dad reminded me that he cut my umbilical cord. I was born at home.

"For our citizenship is in heaven, from which we eagerly wait for a Savior, the Lord Jesus Christ."
(Philippians 3:20 NIV)

I bought wigs, stands, and accessories because my hair is falling out and turning grey. I now embrace this as wisdom and strength. I have earned every grey hair I have, darn it.

"Wisdom belongs to the aged and understanding to the old."
(Job 12:12 NIV)

Chapter 24

The Positive Side Of The Pandemic

I spent a lot of time in God's word.

"All scripture is breathed out by God and profitable for teaching, reproof, and training in righteousness."

(2 Timothy 3:16 NIV)

I got a lot of extra family time. And liked it. We implemented the **"Wheel O Consequence."** That never had a chance! The boxes of "MERCY AND GRACE."

Allow me to explain. Like a box of chocolates, they never knew what they were going to get. The consequences could be washing the car, loss of phone, money off allowance, and cleaning out the cabinets. Mercy and Grace could be money added to allowance, getting out of consequence-free, more phone time, or TV time. However, that lost effectiveness. Time to be prayerful, fair, consistent, and reasonable when issuing them.

Mama Sita is ready to crack down! The file cabinet was color-coded, the cabinets organized, and I became a cleaner person. Practiced social distancing the car from the garage wall (with new bifocals.) Trained my alopecia with my new "Big Sexy Hair" product. Learned unfamiliar words like alopecia (bald spot.)

Chapter 25
A Second Chance To Change Your Final Answer

We are in a country where hate, unemployment, mental health issues, child abuse, domestic violence, and political propaganda are rampant. War, one natural disaster after another, social distancing still seems to be the norm. The Bible talks about the birthing pains of the earth.

"You are going to hear about wars, actual wars, and rumored ones; make sure you do not get alarmed. This has got to happen, but it doesn't mean the end is coming yet, Nations will rise against one another, and there will be famines and earthquakes here and there. All this is just the start of birth pains."

(Matthew 24:6-8 NIV)

I look at the complexity of our bodies. Our blood clots, broken bones heal, the brain signals our heart to pump, oxygen to our lungs, and move our limbs. No one has the same fingerprints or DNA. Not even twins. The trees, galaxies, planets, clouds, and stars are not the same. Is there a God? What if this is my second chance to change my definitive answer? Get right with God. Does it really matter? YES! It is a matter of life and death. As well as where you will spend eternity.

"If it is disagreeable in your sight to serve the Lord, choose today whom you will serve; whether the Gods of your father's house which is beyond the river, or the Gods of the Amorites in whose land you are living, but as for me and my household we will serve the Lord."

(Joshua 14:15 NIV)

MY CHALLENGE

What are you going to choose?

THE MORAL

No matter what you step in, keep walking along singing God's praises. Because God is good all the time and all the time God is good.

"Because your love is better than life, my lips will praise you as long as I live. And in your name, I will lift my hands."

(Psalm 63:3-4 NIV)

UPDATES

Invitations to renew our wedding vows are in the mail. We are renewing ten years of marriage on our anniversary.

Head Rascal has come a long way in his struggle with anger. Feeling empathy for Rascal. Making sure he has food, clothes, etc. I am healing from a lifetime of anxiety and fear. I do not have cancer.

Love Bug and Rascal are young adults now. They are graduating high school. Love Bug is struggling with self-esteem. Learning does not come easy for her.

Rascal got accepted into transitional living and moved into his apartment the day his funding for residential treatment ended. Talk about God's timing!

He is doing well in school and still has accountability. They do a bed check. Rascal has been working at Dairy Queen for a year. He came to church with us the past few Sundays. We played games and healing took place. We focused on four-year colleges. He said he should have listened to me.

"Why are you being so nice to me?" Rascal asked.

"Regardless of what has been said or done you are still my kid," was my answer.

Stay Tuned!

There may be a sequel. I am still a work in progress.

"He who has begun a good work in you will complete it until the day of Jesus Christ."

(Philippians 1:6 NIV)

About The Author

My name is Rebecca Kilwin, and I am known by many aliases. Here is a sample of them: aka Beck, Beckster, Becky, Becky Boo, Becks.

I was born and raised in St. Louis MO. I am a child of God! We are called to share our testimonies in Matthew 5:16, "Let your light shine before men, that they may see your good deeds and praise your Father in Heaven."

I am passionate about my relationship with God. Giving people hope in a fallen world. I felt compelled to be open and honest about my journey. My mentor was my grandmother. I love to scrapbook and have found the beauty of the dollar store. Thank you for allowing me to share my story.

Made in the USA
Monee, IL
02 February 2025

11410793R10059